Here to Help

POSTMAN

Hannah Phillips

Photography by Bobby Humphrey

W
FRANKLIN WATTS

Franklin Watts
Published in Great Britain in 2017 by the Watts Publishing Group

Credits
Series Editors: Hannah Phillips and Paul Humphrey
Series Designer: D. R. ink
Photographer: Bobby Humphrey
Produced for Franklin Watts by Discovery Books Ltd.
Picture credits:
All photographs are by Bobby Humphrey with the exception of: Shutterstock: page 5 (top)
Michael Rosak, page 5 (bottom) KariDesign, Page 14 Whytock, Page 15 (bottom) Evgeny
Karandaev, Page 17 Featureflash/Shutterstock.com.

Every attempt has been made to clear copyright. Should there be any inadvertent
omission please apply to the publisher for rectification.

Dewey number 383.4'9'41
ISBN: 978 1 4451 4004 9

Printed in China

Franklin Watts
An imprint of
Hachette Children's Group
Part of the Watts Publishing Group
Carmelite House
50 Victoria Embankment
London EC4Y 0DZ

An Hachette UK company
www.hachette.co.uk

www.franklinwatts.co.uk

The publisher and packager would like to thank the following people for their help with
this book: Shaun Macken, the Ecclestone family, Michael Neil, Val Bodden and all the
staff at Telford sorting office.

Contents

Words in **bold** are in the glossary on page 24.

I am a postman

Hello, my name is Shaun and I am a postman.

Hello!

?

What is your postman or postwoman's name?

I work for the **Royal Mail**. We deliver lots of letters and **parcels** to people every day.

The letters and parcels we deliver are called '**post**' or '**mail**'.

Starting work

I start work very early in the morning at 6:00am. The big Royal Mail lorries are already at the **delivery office**. They bring post to the delivery office every day so we can deliver it to **local** people.

I swipe my **security** badge on the card reader so I can get into the delivery office.

Why does the postman have a security badge?

Some of the other postal workers are already here.

Sorting the mail

I use a trolley to bring in some of the mail from one of the delivery lorries.

There is lots of post today.

Now I can put the post into area order. This will make it easier for me to sort it out into street order.

I take some post over to the sorting slots. There are slots for every street in my town.

These letters are going to Mountview Road, so I place them here. We have to look at the addresses carefully so we put them in the right slot.

MOUNTVIEW ROAD

Letters can have a **first-class stamp** or a **second-class stamp** on them.

1ST

2ND

?

Which will arrive sooner, a letter with a first- or a second-class stamp?

Getting ready to go

I've finished sorting the mail so I put it all into mailbags.

I collect my van keys and sign for my **special delivery** parcels. We sign for them so we know who is delivering them. Sometimes they contain **valuable** items.

I collect a **scanner** before I leave. People will sign their names on it when I deliver their special delivery parcels.

Phil also works as a postman here. We go out in the same van because our **rounds** are in the same area. We load the van together. We have to make sure that we wear our **reflective** jackets.

? Why do you think postal workers wear reflective jackets on their rounds?

First deliveries

We arrive at the first street and get our mailbags out of the van.

The letters in my mailbag are all in order because I sorted them earlier.

I go to the first house I'm delivering to. I check each address carefully to make sure I post the right letters through the right door.

I push the letters through the letterbox.

Then I go to the next house. There are lots of letters for this one.

In you go!

?

Where is your letterbox? Why is it important to make sure the letters are pushed through the letterbox carefully?

Safety

It's important for me to stay safe while I'm out delivering. Pet dogs live in lots of houses. Most dogs are friendly, but some of them aren't.

BEWARE OF DOG

I use a **posting stick** to put the mail through the door. This stops me from getting any nasty dog bites.

I also have to make sure that I'm protected from the Sun. I wear sun cream and a hat if it's hot. I keep water with me to make sure that I stay **hydrated** in hot weather.

Birthday parcel

There are balloons tied up outside the next house. It is somebody's birthday.

?

Have you ever received a birthday parcel in the post? What was in it?

Happy birthday!

I have birthday cards and a parcel for Storm. She is nine today. She is very excited about what might be in her parcel.

I deliver lots of birthday cards and parcels to people.

People who reach their 100th birthday get a card from Buckingham Palace. Inside is a birthday message from the Queen.

Special deliveries

I have two special deliveries. These are important and people must sign for them.

I knock on the door and ask the lady who lives there to sign on the scanner. This sends information back to the office to let them know the parcel has been delivered.

I knock on another door but there is nobody in. This special delivery will need to go back to the office.

I fill out a card to tell the person who lives here that I tried to deliver it.

I deliver a postcard to the next house.

? Who has sent the postcard? Where have they gone on holiday?

Back to the delivery office

Now we've finished our rounds, it's time to go back to the delivery office.

How did your round go today, Phil?

I hand the special delivery package back in so it can be put in a safe place.

I put my mailbags away ready for the next day.

?

Why was the special delivery item brought back to the delivery office?

I check my hours on the **duties board** to see what **shifts** I'm working for the rest of the week.

It is 2:00pm and time for me to go home now.

Helping people

I really enjoy my job as a postman. I enjoy being active and working outside. Most of all, I enjoy making sure that people get their post delivered on time.

I really enjoy helping people!

When you grow up...

If you would like to be a postman or postwoman, here are some simple tips and advice:

What kind of person are you?

- You are friendly and helpful
- You are active and enjoy walking
- You are polite and well mannered
- You pay attention and can remember lots of details
- You enjoy being outside.

How do you become a postman or postwoman?

You don't need any special qualifications to become a postman or postwoman. You have to register online and take a test. You may then be asked for an interview and have to pass a security test before you can start delivering letters.

Answers

P7. The postman has a security badge because there are valuable items inside the delivery office.

P9. A letter with a first-class stamp will arrive sooner than one with a second-class stamp.

P11. Postal workers wear reflective jackets so they can easily be seen and because it is often dark when they start work.

P13. It is important to push the letters through the letterbox carefully because their contents can get damaged.

P19. Grandma and Grandpa sent the postcard. They went to Greece for their holiday.

P21. Special delivery items cannot be left on the doorstep because they may contain valuable items. They are brought back to the delivery office for safekeeping.

Were your answers the same as the ones in this book? Don't worry if they were different, sometimes there is more than one right answer. Talk about your answer with other people. Can you explain why you think your answer is right?

Glossary

delivery office the place where the post is brought to be sorted, ready for delivery

duties board a board that has all the times and days when postal workers have to work

first-class stamp this stamp is used for post that needs to be delivered quickly

hydrated to keep a healthy balance in your body by drinking enough water, especially when it's hot outside

local describes the area close to where you live

mail another word for post

parcel a larger item of post, usually too big to go through a letterbox

post the letters and parcels that postal workers deliver

posting stick a safety stick used to post letters to houses that may have dangerous dogs

reflective describes the material on clothing that reflects light so people can be seen at all times.

round the delivery route that a postman or postwoman does every day

Royal Mail a company that delivers the post all across the UK

scanner an electronic device that is used to collect signatures from people who have special deliveries

second-class stamp this stamp is used for post that does not have to be delivered quickly

security describes something that is used to keep a person or a place safe

shift the period of time when a postal worker has to work

special delivery important post that has to be signed for

valuable describes the post that might be very important or be worth a lot of money

Index